ALL MIRACLE

Storing September

April 9, 1924–February 16, 1999

ALL MIRACLE

Storing September

Poems by
Elizabeth B. Rooney

Edited by
Patricia M. Rooney

Brigham Farm Publishing

Published by Brigham Farm Publishing
2990 Cave of the Mounds Road
Blue Mounds, WI 53517
www.brighamfarm.com

Cover photo is by Jim Becia © 1997. For more information
about his photographs, check www.spiritlightphotography.com.

Interior artwork © 2001 Simone Portia McLoughlin

Cover and book design by Elizabeth Ragsdale

Quote by Luci Shaw in preface is used with permission of
the author.

Library of Congress Control Number: 2001119946

ISBN 0-9716001-0-4 (set of four)
ISBN 0-9716001-1-2 (v. 1)
ISBN 0-9716001-2-0 (v. 2)
ISBN 0-9716001-3-9 (v. 3)
ISBN 0-9716001-4-7 (v. 4)

*To the women of the Society of
the Companions of the Holy Cross
and all of Mom's praying companions
who encouraged her along the way.*

ALL MIRACLE SERIES
Elizabeth B. Rooney

Morning Song

Packages

Storing September

Gift Wrapped

Contents

PREFACE   xi

ACKNOWLEDGMENTS   xv

Autumn   xvi

   Storing September   1

September   2

October   36

November   70

Epitaph   103

September

September Gift   3

School Bus   4

Industrious   5

Picnic   6

Cricket   7

Sharing   8

Rooster   9

Sidelights   10

Late Marriage   11

Gentle Night   12

Christian Soldier   13

To the Creator   14

Night Roses   15

Careless   16

Satellite   17

Promenade   18

Encounter   19

Fruiting   20

Harvest   21

Night Sky   22

Friend Moon   23

Traveler   24

Presence   25

Owl   26

Trapped   27

Valedictory   28

Golden Gift   29

Benediction   30

Acceptance   31

Calendar   32

Where? Why? When?   34

October

Unique   37
Benignus   38
Peronne-Marie   39
Virginia at Ninety   40
Widow   41
Hands   42
Youth   43
Insight   44
Vintage Verse   45
On the Wearing of Purple   46
So Many Years   47
To Be Bereaved   48
Holy Matrimony   49
Loneliness   50
Defiant   51
Aging   52
Forced Retirement   53
Growing Older   54
Autumn   55
"Old Age Is Not for Sissies"   56
Useless?   58
Generation Gap   59
Futures   60
Distance   61
Outdated   62
Reversal   63
Marooned   64
For Care Givers   65
Old Woman   66
Miss Havisham   67
Bitter Lot   68
Questions   69

November

Wild Geese   71
Closing   72
Safety Net   73
Hunted   74
Prodigal   75
A Timeless Marvel   76
Repentance   77
Adamant   78
Mercy   79
Rescued   80
Comforter   81
All There Is   82
Making Amends   83
Fish Wife   84
Appeal   85
Anonymous   86
Establishment   87
Lawyer   88
Person in Her Own Right   89
Busybody   90
Isolated   91
Friend in Need   92
Suicide   93
Deserted   94
Grief   95
Farm Dog   96
Sharing   97
Absence   98
Grieving   99
Waking Alone   100
November   101

Preface

This series of books is for all of Elizabeth Rooney's family, friends and fans who have been patiently awaiting the publication of her collected poems and for all those who will meet her for the first time in these pages.

Elizabeth Brigham Rooney, my mother, began writing poems in the summer of 1978. Before her death in February 1999, she had written over seven hundred of them, interspersed amongst the prose entries in her journals like bursts of song.

She was more surprised than anyone at this sudden and abundant release of creativity, although she'd been encouraged from her youth to pursue a career in writing. Raised by highly literate parents, she attended and excelled at top-notch schools, yet protested, "I don't have anything to say!"

Later, she came to realize the creative flow had been blocked, among other things, by fear of failing those who expected so much from her. It wasn't until she made a complete surrender to the One who had placed the love of poetry inside her that she was free, not only to write but also to embrace all of life as a holy gift.

This "total commitment," as she described it, came as she was preparing to be inducted into the Society of the Companions of the Holy Cross, a lay order of Episcopal women. She already had her masters in Christian Education and was married to an Episcopal priest, yet there was something missing.

"For years I'd been an active Christian adult and before that, a rather timid, but believing child. I prayed quite regularly for as long as I can remember, but at the same time stayed a safe distance from the cross. To embrace the cross wholeheartedly requires an act of will. To my astonishment, the result was an absolute flooding of joy. I had fallen in love with God. It was as if my veins were bubbling with champagne and the poems began to flow freely, coming as delightful surprises day after day."

The first one to come was "Adelynrood," named for the retreat center in Massachusetts where the encounter took place.

Adelynrood

The winter of my heart
Melts here.
Rivulets run
Beneath the ice of fear.

Pierced by your warmth,
Life moves.
Spring has begun.
I feel the sun, the sun!

8/11/78

As her newly awakened faith grew, so did the conviction that these poems were gifts to be shared. She summoned the courage to exchange poetry with friends who were fellow writers. Then she attended a workshop led by the poet Luci Shaw and there found a kindred heart and mind, a friend and mentor, who eventually introduced her to the reading public in a way Elizabeth never dreamed possible.

Luci had been asked to write a chapter in an upcoming book entitled *Bright Legacy, Portraits of Ten Outstanding Christian Women* about someone she "particularly admired." As Luci explains in her chapter, "Rather then telling of the impact on my life of an internationally known personality, I felt a growing conviction that I would rather talk about someone like Elizabeth Rooney, an 'ordinary' woman, hardly known beyond her own circle of friends and colleagues, though uniquely gifted by God. Her experience would, I was sure, suggest to other women with earthbound, unremarkable lives that he could lift the most mundane existence into his own bright beauty and glory. What he requires are eyes open to his brightness and ears alert for his voice."

Luci's words so aptly describe the gift Elizabeth received at Adelynrood. She had indeed been given "eyes open to his brightness and ears alert for his voice." And so the woman who had protested she had nothing to write about, was able to declare, "I know what I want to say. . . . I want to write about God, about the intense tenderness manifest in the world wherever goodness, truth and beauty allow it to shine through… Today in the parking lot there was a puddle—a muddy, shallow puddle on the blacktop, not more than an inch deep at best and perhaps four feet across. When looked at from a certain angle, it reflected all the treetops in it, and clouds and sky, all the way to infinity. I think I'm like the puddle—muddy, shallow, insignificant—but, by God's grace, capable of the miracle of reflecting him, and in him, all the wonder of the universe.

"The more I become aware of the active presence of God, the more beautiful and sacred everything becomes.... Do we need miracles, or do we need only to perceive that every ordinary thing around us is already miraculous?"

My mother's hope, as voiced in the following prayer by an unknown author, was that her poems might open other eyes to His brightness and other ears to His voice, that they would come to understand as she had that "Life is *all* miracle."

"Days pass and the years vanish and we walk sightless among miracles. Lord, fill our eyes with seeing and our minds with knowing. Let there be moments when your Presence, like lightning, illumines the darkness in which we walk. Help us to see, wherever we gaze, that the bush burns unconsumed. And we, clay touched by God, will reach out for holiness and exclaim in wonder, 'How filled with awe is this place and we did not know it.'"

《 》

This series, *All Miracle*, includes four volumes, *Morning Song, Packages, Storing September*, and *Gift Wrapped*, which correspond to spring, summer, autumn, and winter. Those who, like my mother, have grown up on farms or in the country understand and interpret life, in large part, by the passage of the seasons. Her poetry is characterized by a deep awareness of life's interconnectedness and the yearly cycles of death and rebirth. After much reading and rereading of the poems, I felt the most natural way to group them would be by these intrinsic themes, which include not only the four seasons but also the parallel seasons of human life, such as childhood, adulthood, aging, and death and the corresponding seasons of the liturgical year, such as Advent, Christmas, Lent, and Easter. Although each poem is meant to be read and savored on its own, the groupings are intended to accentuate their collective rhythm and flow.

—*Patricia M. Rooney*

Acknowledgments

My most sincere thanks to the following persons and companies:

To all who helped launch this publishing venture by generously contributing to the Elizabeth B. Rooney Memorial Poetry Fund.

To Eugenia Brown, who so cheerfully volunteered hours and hours of typing.

To Louise Summers, Delores Topliff, Pat Hitchcock, Norma Madsen, Sharol Hayner, Joyce Young, Kimberly Linyard, Janice Griffin, and Sr. Peronne-Marie Thiebert, for their gracious help with proofreading.

To my brother Mark, for all of his encouragement, advice, and nagging.

To the wonderful folks at Impressions Book and Journal Services, Inc., especially John Ferguson, Mary Boss, and Elizabeth Ragsdale, for their expertise, enthusiasm, and genuine interest in this project. Your patience and warmth working with a first-time publisher made all the difference.

To Kevin Wasowski and Jane Landen of Edwards Brothers, for their kind and professional help.

Autumn

This benign weather—this gentle, golden Fall! A sunset last night like a great, rose-colored wing curved over the edge of the world . . . there was a patch of Queen Anne's lace and clover shadowed against the setting sun that overflowed my heart with beauty. . . . As I have been writing, the sun has come over the horizon and the eastern side of every leaf and branch and tree trunk is glistening with gold. I feel like that. I'm the same branch, the same twig, but to the extent that I allow myself to be suffused with God as the trees are with sunlight, to that extent I am transformed, golden and glistening. And I don't have to do anything, anymore than the trees do, except stay in the same place and make myself be still and let Him come. . . .

Journal, 9/22/78

*S*toring *S*eptember

You ask me what I did today.
I could pretend and say,
"I don't remember."
But, no, I'll tell you what I did today—
I stored September.
Sat in the sun and let the sun sink in,
Let all the warmth of it caress my skin.
When winter comes, my skin will still remember
The day I stored September.
And then my eyes—
I filled them with the deepest, bluest skies
And all the traceries of wasps and butterflies.
When winter comes, my eyes will still remember
The day they stored September.
And there was cricket song to fill my ears!
And the taste of grapes
And the deep purple of them!
And asters, like small clumps of sky . . .
You know how much I love them.
That's what I did today
And I know why.
Just simply for the love of it,
I stored September.

9/25/90

September

September Gift

I wish that I could pick
This autumn day for you,
Could gather up
A bright bouquet for you
Of asters, oak trees,
Maples, butterflies
With handfuls, armfuls
Of these blue, blue skies.

9/25/87

School Bus

The bright yellow box full of children
Moves through the morning
Gathering in the smiles,
The warm hands.
Each carries our love
Wrapped in wax paper,
Carefully hoarded till noon.

How little we know
Of the mystery dwelling within them,
Of what is beginning to grow.
Know only that we must send them
Out to wait by the mail box,
Up the steps into the bus—
Trusting life's unpredictable afternoon
To bring them back to us.

10/4/79

Industrious

I am a spider,
Spinning threads of thought.
Gossamer bits float off,
Are carried by the breeze . . .
Some stay
And can become a web of words
Entrapping fancies
Or the morning dew.
My work
Is weaving wonderment for you.

6/9/79

Picnic

Two grasshoppers
Had lunch with me,
A butterfly
And one small bee.

We broke our bread
Beneath the sun
One autumn day
At just past one.

The asters
And the goldenrod
Joined us
In giving thanks to God

For food
And for good company—
The flowers, the wingéd ones
And me.

9/24/88

Cricket

A cricket
Creaked and cricketed
Across the path
In front of me.
His earnest progress
Zigged and zagged
Because he was
So crickety!

8/17/78

Sharing

The wasp and I
Are lazy in the autumn sun.
Why hurry?
Winter seems so far away.
Yes, we both know
That frost will come
But, for today,
We browse about
Soaking up all the light
We come upon.
We fumble, bumble,
Brush against each other
But not in anger.
I do not swat
Nor am I stung.
Today there's warmth enough
For all of us.
Isn't there,
Little brother!

9/30/92

Rooster

You strut in the grass behind me
Gargling threats
And trying to peck my legs.
Red-wattled and magnificent,
You are all arrogance and bluff.
You do not seem to remember
The ball of fluff
I held in my hand last spring.
You think of yourself
As a lord, as a ruler, a king,
Husbanding all your harem of hens.
Cock of the walk, of the farm, of the land,
You are fierce and feathered and grand.
But don't ask me
To scuttle meekly off
Like some fat hen.
I knew you when.

11/16/81

Sidelights

The setting sun
Looked back at the little town
And sent its love.
Long lines of light
Mellowed and warmed the roofs.
A kind of softness overlay the earth.
The barns turned pink,
The cornfields, lavender,
And all the windows blazed with sudden fire.
The loveliness made love perceptible—
A glory we could see and almost touch.
Even when dark came on, the gentle gray
Recalled the wonder of the end of day.

10/29/79

Late Marriage

The new house faces west.
After the years of turmoil,
They have found
A refuge in these hills
And in each other.
Here they can turn their backs
On the long morning of their lives
With all its pain.
All they have left
Is life's late afternoon.
As night begins to stain
The western sky,
They hope the sunset
Will not come too soon.

5/27/94

Gentle Night

The night is quiet,
Filled with cricket song.
The brown dogs pad about,
Noses patrol the air.
Out in the moonlit woods
Small creatures start and quiver.
Tires move quietly along the road.
The family sleep,
And moonlight blesses everything.
Good night.

8/23/78

Christian Soldier

Armored in gossamer, I stand
Amid a valiant throng.
Entrenched
Against the forces of the night
With poetry and song.

8/15/78

To the Creator

Oh, your moon is so beautiful, Lord!
And your stars—
The faint pricks in the darkening sky!
And that low ring of rose
Spreading out from the vanishing sun,
A last scarf of light left by day
Just as night was begun.
Every moment
You're making new loveliness, Lord,
And You never get done!

9/24/90

Night Roses

Suddenly night bloomed
And stars like great white roses
Filled the sky.

4/1/94

Careless

I haven't cleaned the cellar,
I forgot to sweep the stair,
There's a button off my jacket,
Jonny's blue jeans have a tear,
There's an old arthritic lady
Whom I should uphold in prayer,
And I'm sitting in the moonlight,
The moonlight, the moonlight,
Adoring You by moonlight,
As if I had no care!

4/16/79

Satellite

It ticked its way
Across the sky.
As busy as the hand
Recording seconds on a watch,
It moved above the land.

The face of that immensity
Lay still from dark to dawn
Except where man's presumption
Intruded and was gone.

5/15/79

Promenade

The moon's out walking a star
On a string,
Just one small, brilliant,
Star-bright thing
In all that wilderness of sky.

Star trails the moon
From cloud to cloud
While moon,
Proprietary, proud,
Travels the whole, wide
Breadth of night
Exploring heaven by moonlight.

11/4/87

Encounter

I stand beneath a night of stars
And see
As far as I can look
Into infinity.
I kneel at the communion rail
And meet
That very infinite
Come down to me—
His flesh to be part of my flesh,
His blood to flow with mine,
His love come from beyond
Creation's farthest sky
As bread and wine.

1/28/79

Fruiting

We have come round again
To moon and mist
And cricket song at night.
The tasseled corn stands deep,
The grapes are ripe,
And I stand wondering
Whether, in all this harvest of delight,
I have allowed His fruit
To grow in me,
Fruit of the Spirit
Grown invisibly.

8/28/85

Harvest

Dark of the night,
The sweet stars bending
Like golden grain
In the arching sky.

Dark of the moon,
A crescent swinging,
A reaper's blade
To mow them by.

Sickle-sharp,
It will cut its way
Through the harvest of stars
Till the new-born day

Gathers the golden
Sheaves of light
And hides them away
For another night.

1/17/83

Night Sky

Orion and one pine,
Night and star shine!
Patches of white cloud glowing, blowing,
Wind like coldest water flowing.

One cloud blows through the Dipper.
Does it leak?
Comes thence the coldness going past my cheek?
It is the slip stream of the earth, this cold
Whose fingers fit my body like a mold.

On such a night,
I would put on Orion's belt
And play
Catch with the wisps of cloud
Until the day.

Dry leaves go whispering across the dirt
Rustling and hollow
Like the trailing skirt
Of dance and poetry and song.

I must lie back on the earth's breast and sleep
Small, warm and surfeited
With beauty.

1/5/59

Friend Moon

Old moon,
Of course we gave you a face.
We've watched you
Swimming the seas of space
Or wrapping yourself
In clouds of lace.
We've seen you
Tending the stars like sheep
And felt you
Bright on the face of sleep.
You've watched us love,
And you've watched us weep.
At every age
And in every place,
You share our lives
And you share our space.
Old moon,
Of course we gave you a face.

9/1/90

Traveler

The world turns slowly.
Silent, branch by branch,
The harvest moon
Climbs the long ladder
Of the evening sky.
The twigs draw faces
On the golden ghost
Until the pale mask
Frees itself above them.

We rest our consciences
On wheeling earth
And wake to find moon
Tired and pale
Beginning to climb down
Our western windows.
It's taken her all night
Just to get over our small roof
While I have traveled
Half the world in dreams.
Moon's journey
Must be longer than it seems.

11/15/78

Presence

Deep, deep
Within the moon-filled woods
Where midnight shadows
Stream across the snow,
The deer of autumn move
Invisible
To all but memory.

So you,
Whom I no longer touch
Or see,
Come stepping quietly
And stand
Within the shelter of my heart.

Oh, love,
I miss you
When we are apart.

1/19/88

Owl

Now,
In the silent hour before dawn,
Hour of darkness,
Hour of desire,
The westward waning moon
Casts pale green fire.

A great horned owl
Calls in the wood.
His "Hoo—Hoo, hoohoo"
Carries foreboding, fright,
And all the mysteries
Of dark, of night.

I, who am civilized,
Still feel
The pricking of my hair
Against my skin
And look for signs
That day will soon begin.

10/4/82

Trapped

Run, mouse!
Quick!
Scurry, worry, hurry, hide!
The golden god runs up the eastern sky,
Fiercer than cat and fleeter!
Is there no darkness left?
No crack, no hole?
No crevice, cranny, burrow?
Even inside myself
No refuge anymore?
Everything open wide?
A mouse can't live in such a world.
No coward can!
Must I be gilded then
And made a man?

9/22/78

Valedictory

All of the bushes are burning now!
All of the trees are aflame!
The woods are alive with the glory of God,
And the leaves are telling His name!

Sighing, whispering, fluttering friends,
For weeks they have given us breath.
Dying now as the summer ends,
They defy the sadness of death!
They fling their color before the world
With the unleashed joy of a flag unfurled.

Praising the Maker of summer thunder,
Praising the sunshine, praising the wonder
Of velvet night and of flaming morning,
They hail the Lord in this last adorning
Of radiant color before they utter
A final sigh and begin to flutter
Back to the earth where at last they die
So other springs can touch the sky.

10/19/78

Golden Gift

I will remember
How the flakes of fall
Came spinning, spinning
Down the shafts of light.
Pieces of gold
New-minted by the frost,
Tree treasure
Tossed across the gleaming morning
By the breeze,
God's golden gift, these memories
Will warm us
When the world turns crystal cold.

10/11/91

Benediction

The tall trees
Shed their yellow leaves
Like blessings
Upon the bride and groom.
Their gold leaf
Drifts across the golden air
Here in this outdoor room.
May you be blessed, be blessed
The tall trees murmur
Adding their benediction
To our prayers.
Like us, the tall trees
Celebrate the union
Of this beloved pair.

10/29/91

Acceptance

Hoarding the sun
Among the mists of fall,
Watching the leaves spin down,
I hear the call
Of God within my heart.

Fruiting is almost past.
I watch the branches
Cast aside
The last debris of summer.

The birds know
As they gather on the wires,
Planning to flee
Before the warmth expires.

This is the dying time,
The time to say goodbye,
To accept the life
That has been lived
And not to ask for more
Or wonder why.

9/29/88

Calendar

Is life, then,
Only pages on a wall—
A grid of numbered squares
Bounded by sleep, by prayers?

A breeze comes in the window . . .
Pages fall
Like autumn leaves,
Spring petals, winter flakes.
Minutes are so minute.
We do not notice how each makes
An imperceptible addition to our past.
We look around at last
And they have all
Drifted away,
Leaving a blank space on the faded wall
Like a memorial plaque
Commemorating life.

We remember the fluttering pages.
We reach with uncertain fingers
Wanting them back,
But they have withered, melted,
Or been raked away.
Somehow,
We had never imagined
That they would not stay.

8/14/81

Where? Why? When?

Where do you come from, wind?
Where are you going?
What is the haste behind
This blowing and blowing?
You've almost blown September away.
All that's left is a single day.
Minute by minute, it's going, too.
We hug time close
And then you go, "Whoooo!"
And all of our moments
Sail off in the blue.
Will there come a time
When I sail off, too?

9/30/95

October

Unique

You were
One golden leaf
In this great autumn harvest
Of your kind.

You were so small
Among the million, million
Leaves of fall,
Yet when you trembled from the branch
And circling came,
One tiny evanescent piece of flame,
You were not just the same
As all the other leaves
Because my heart
Had learned to know your name.

10/20/87

Benignus

Too honest to deceive herself,
Too brave to hide,
Too daring to protect herself
From those who have denied
Her love,
Too caring . . .
She has grown
Wiser, more passionate.

She has become
Not weary worn
But honed.
Her skin lies closer to the bone.
You feel the quality
Of polished wood or stone—
Polished by discipline,
By fasting and by prayer,
By willingness to let life hurt
And still be altogether there.

4/25/81

Peronne-Marie

Like a great stone outcropping
Clothed in trees,
The strength concealed
Beneath the outer beauty,
So you appear to me.

Meeting you, I encounter love,
And gentleness and laughter.
Your wisdom and your generosity
Show clearly as we talk.
It's only after
We've been together for awhile
That I perceive
How your habitual caring
Has disciplined your strength.
Yes, you are rock,
A woman others lean on, look to, love,
And choose to lead them.

6/16/96

Virginia at Ninety

Who fear not death
Can even age enjoy.
Proud hearts,
They fly their courage
Fearlessly.
Theirs is the beauty
Only weathering
Can bring to wood
Or to the human face.
The long, brave years
Produce their harvest now
In gallantry and grace.

9/20/79

Widow

She is a white rose—
Full blown,
The vernal crispness
Turning soft,
Her heart still golden,
While her beauty's fragrance
Grows richer
With the poignancy of sorrow.
Children and friends
Gather
Like autumn butterflies,
Each feeding on the nectar
Of her kindness.

3/3/79

Hands

A woman's hands, my hands!
In over sixty years,
They've learned so much—
Just how to ease a shirt
Over a small child's head,
The swiftest, smoothest way
To make a bed.
They know exactly how
Well-kneaded dough should feel,
Can thread a needle,
Grasp a steering wheel.
Knowing and capable
Yet gentle in their touch,
These hands have felt so much.

8/13/89

Youth

Mine was a young face once.
I see them now—
So bland, so inexperienced,
So new,
The personality
Not yet come through.
Vulnerable they are
And sensitive,
Especially the eyes.
But it takes years
To grow compassionate
And wise.

8/6/87

Insight

My old eyes blur.
The figure crucified
Against the distant wall
Is harder to distinguish
Now.
Yet deep within my heart
That figure burns
More clearly,
Sharp
And luminous with love.

The passing of the years
That dimmed my sight
Has made my inner vision
More intense, more bright.

5/5/88

Vintage Verse

Old, am I?
Well, the question is—
What's "old" convey to you?
By old, do you mean worn out,
Useless, ready to discard
As in "old shoe"?
Or do you mean "old"
Like an antique table or a vase,
Something that has been cherished
Through the years,
Shined, polished, valued
For its workmanship and grace.
Some things improve with age—
Wisdom and souls and wine.
Before you brush me off
Because I'm "old",
Come and taste mine.

7/5/93

On the Wearing of Purple

When I am an old woman,
I shall wear purple
Because it is the badge of royalty.
When I am old enough,
I will become the true ruler of myself,
A sovereignty hard won.
I will share wisdom, courage, joy
With the still struggling young—
But only if I have learned how to die
To wants and needs and selfishness and greed.
And only if I have learned very deeply
Exactly who I am.
I will have to learn to overcome my pride,
To set all jealousy and sham aside.
When I am old,
I will be beautiful—
But only if I let Love teach me how to love,
Only if I spend years growing like Him.
You may or may not notice
How white my hair has grown,
And that my eyes are dim,
But you will notice
That I am become
Royal enough so that I can wear purple
With gold
And a touch of ermine in the trim.

5/12/92

So Many Years

How gently
You have dealt with us,
Dear Lord!
How swiftly
Time has flown!

When we were young
And very much in love,
We had our dreams
Of growing old together.
And now, we have grown old
And find ourselves
Still very much in love.

Thank you for every moment
We have known,
For all we share.
Glad in You,
We go forward hand in hand,
Trusting each other
To Your love and care.

7/4/93 for 7/3/93 *(Dad's birthday)*

To Be Bereaved

He brings the world alive!
Without him,
I would slow down
Imperceptibly.
I doubt that I would die
Physically, outwardly
(Though I might wish I could
And know that wish as sin),
But somewhere, deep within,
Part of me would have died—
The part that laughed at his bright wit,
The part that sang when he came in the door,
The part that liked to have him in the room
And felt a deep content when he was near,
The part that has not learned to live alone
After so many years together here.

6/20/90

Holy Matrimony

I took you, love,
In sickness or in health,
For better or for worse
And now I live my promise out.

Charmed with each other's youth,
We could not know
That someday
You would drool and shuffle
And forget your words
While I would keep
My warmth and wit and swiftness.

I use them now to cherish you,
To wrap you round with gentleness
And patient courtesy.
I love you, dear.
All the goods you have been to me
Still halo you.
The promises we made
Hold and support us both.
We are each other's cross,
Each other's greatest blessing.

9/1/78

Loneliness

The loneliness slants across the grass,
Creeps from behind the wood
And swallows down
The last bright bits of day.

Busy with food and news
And the family's needs,
I am usually defended
Against the sadness that steals
Through the windows and out the walls
When they've all gone away.

I need their nearness, their warmth,
The sight and sound of each one,
To affirm me, to make me alive to myself,
To give me the courage to stay.

8/21/93

Defiant

You see it sometimes in old trees—
The twisted pine crouching against the cliff,
A lonely oak with jagged stumps of limbs.
A curious gnarled courage
Still stirs the sap in spring,
Old roots still cling.

The old man limps across the parking lot.
He is, "Fine, fine except for my hip, of course."
He wants to write a book about the way
Things have changed during his life,
About the decay
He sees around him but denies within.
If only he could find the words,
He would begin . . .

9/18/80

Aging

An old dog now,
His muzzle graying
And his coat
Less silken to the touch.

He wanted to go to the beach with us,
Running and leaping about
As he always had.
The crying of gulls and the breeze
And the foam round his feet
Always drove him half mad.

Now we made him stay in
By the fire
With his chin on his paws.
He kept trying to tell us
That we were breaking his heart.

We only intended to keep him
From hurting himself.
He could barely manage to walk,
And certainly not all that way,
But the grief in his eyes
Kept haunting me
All through the day.

8/4/93

Forced Retirement

It's hard for an old man
To say, "Goodbye."
He confuses his manliness
With the things he's done.
Tragic as Lear,
He has to surrender his throne.

Of course, there's the cottage
Up north,
And he's always wanted to fish,
Never really had time for fishing before . . .
But what do you do
After the fishing is through?

It's hard for an old man
To say, "Goodbye."
Especially when he wishes
That things were just the way
They used to be
Before they made him,
As they put it, free.

For him there's so much dying
In this act
That he may really die
And be too proud
To understand just why.

3/17/86

Growing Older

She had been like bone china—
Exquisite,
But now her hand lay on my arm
Fragile as eggshell.
She had been independent,
Determined still to be
Erect and separate
And free,
But now she leaned on me.
We longed to comfort her
But she denied each day's dilapidation,
Scaffolded in pride.

11/13/89

Autumn

The fragile perish first.
Petals and butterflies and birds
All leave us now.
Our days have drunk up
All earth's warmth.
We swallow dust
And shuffle through dead leaves.
The bleak, the cold,
The bitter dregs of fall
Give sorry solace.

Seeking our summer youth,
We thumb torn pages
Only to find their beauty
Fly-specked, faded.
The truth we thought we knew
Has shredded and grown tattered
And even love's worn thin
From constant fingering.
A miserable business
This long lingering!

9/29/78

"Old Age Is Not for Sissies"

The lonely courage
Of the old
Is seldom noticed,
Seldom told.

We who are young
Forget that they
Must frequently
Sit still all day.

Our lives are filled
With people who
May reach their graves
Before we do,

Leaving us loveless,
Lonely, lost.
Oh, do not minimize
The cost

Of living longer
Than your health,
Your friends, your family,
And your wealth!

Most are too proud,
Too stoic to complain,
But do not underestimate
Their pain.

6/28/81

Useless?

Life has become so slight.
The network holding me
No longer keeps out
All the winds of fear.
I am become like last year's bird's nest—
Useful once, but now
Tousled, frail, broken,
Easily blown down.
They will be building new, strong nests
Next spring
And last year's nests
Will not be good for anything.

9/12/93

Generation Gap

They always seat me in the most comfortable chair.
I am marooned in my best silk print
Like something ancient washed up on a beach.
They gather in little pools of conversation,
Ripples of laughter reach across the rug.
I would have liked a hug
But they are intimidated by the fierceness in me.
They come with cups of coffee and respect.
We send out tentacles of speech,
Trying to penetrate the years
That I have fought through, suffered, loved, endured.
Lovely and inaccessible mirages of myself,
They shimmer before me, draw close, then recede.
How can I speak across the reach of time
The courage they do not yet know they need?

6/8/80

Futures

The winter sunlight touches wrinkled skin.
The lucid lemon warms the ancient blood.
Scarcely perceived, its gentleness caresses
The blue-veined hands resting in quietness
Above the blanket's warmth.
Once the warm-blooded vigor flowed
So hot and swift that sunlight was redundant.
We poured abundant energy and heart
In superfluity on all around us.
Our shells dry slowly.
Now, we sit within our husks,
Waiting and trying to keep warm.
We cherish the vitality of others—
Love, laughter, fire and sunlight, food, caresses.
Remember us, you who are warm and young
With fire to spare.
As you are, we were once.
Think of the years awaiting you
And save us from despair.

9/26/78

Distance

Why must the loved child
Vanish from our sight,
Move half-way round the world,
Or die by some mischance?

Alone in the apartment,
I remember
The warmth of hugs,
The hours laughter lightened.
If love were not so far away,
I would not be so frightened.

2/12/81

Outdated

She waits
As an old piano waits
Her music silent
In the depths of her,
Her varnish cracked and worn.

She had been lovely once,
Beautiful
And responsive to a touch,
A means of magic
To all those who knew her.

Now those who come
Do not know how to play.
They dust her, check her health
And use her to display
Old photographs.

Her music is unheard,
Unsummoned now,
Surrounded though she is
By the sound of their conversation
And their laughs.

10/18/89

Reversal

You were my mother once
And I was child.
You were my mother once,
Omniscient, strong.
Now you have lived so long
I am become
Mother to you
And you, child-like to me.

Yet are you mother still,
Still to be honored, loved,
Shown all respect.
When I was child,
You were kind, brave and true.
May I be such a mother now
To you!

6/4/88

Marooned

Now is the lonely time,
The time of waiting,
Of daily visits to the nursing home
And nights alone.
His things are everywhere around the home
And he, himself, present in all the rooms
Which he has left.
Without intending to,
He's sailed beyond my reach
And I'm left lonely, stranded on the beach
Of our past life together in this place.
How do I make peace with this strange life—
Half widow, half companionable wife?

2/18/91

For Care Givers

Sometimes the very brave
Are hungry, too,
Hungry for comfort,
For encouragement.
They give and give,
Pour out their strength and warmth
In caring love,
And don't say much
About their own fatigue.
Yet they too need to feel
Held, warmed, protected, blessed.
They too need rest.

5/21/92

Old Woman

She looks like death or danger,
Like a killing frost.
The people in her life
Are hesitant to blossom
Fearing blight.

Surely, she was not born like this.
One wonders what dark night,
What deep abyss of terror,
What cold fright
Has chilled her to this look
Of frozen bone.

Christ of compassion,
Can you comfort her?
She seems so desolate,
So locked within herself
And so alone.

2/17/87

Miss Havisham

Still fanning ghosts of flame,
She hunches closer to her empty heart,
Remembers embers where no embers are
And seeks to warm herself
With wraiths of wrath.
The cold ash, stirred,
Brings tear dust to her eyes.
Blinded by bitter years
Of failing to forgive,
She has remembered to hate,
Forgotten to live.

9/11/80

Bitter Lot

It is the drying up of unshed tears
That turns us in the end
To shafts of salt.
The feelings unexpressed all down the years
Precipitate within us
Leaving grief
In layers on our vulnerable souls.

Our hardened hearts
Began as soft and tender as a child's.
After so many wounds,
With so much salt poured into them,
We have grown stiff with pain.

Unable to follow even those we love
Into new lands,
We find we must remain
Stranded in bitterness, irreconciled,
As lonely pillars in a desert wild.

6/17/80

Questions

Friend, will I also
Peer across the years,
My eyes grown dim and rheumy
In their turn?
And will I yearn for youth
And reach to touch a child's smooth cheek
Knowing my withered fingers seek
The firmness and freshness
They have lost?
Will I remain
Cheerful and even bold,
Although I know the cost of growing old?
Or will I fill
With bitterness and rage
Because I am diminished
As I age?

8/7/94

November

Wild Geese

Barking and calling courage to each other,
The singing skein sweeps south across the sky.
We hear their legendary cry
Saying goodbye to summer swamps and sweetness.
They know some ancient mystery of weather,
Of daring and of caring for each other,
Which we have lost.
Shrouded in sheets and city streets,
Our stifled hearts half waken at their sound.
Something within us trembles, flaps its wings,
Falls back against the ground.
We dress for breakfast, start the daily round
And wonder, why we must know only fenced yards,
And shelled corn, until we die?

10/16/78

Closing

Tonight the curtain falls!
The wise have left the theater long ago,
Knowing the play is over.

We who remain
Have each our hoard of summer—
Apples, potatoes, squash, and piles of wood.
The trees have stored their sap;
The bees, their honey.
The ground hog has retreated to his dreams.

Beneath gray-feather clouds,
The earth is turning to iron
And the wind to steel.
Cold bites to the bone.

Is anyone left out in the bitter night
Improvident and shivering and alone?
Dear Lover of lost sheep,
Bring each one home!

11/11/78

Safety Net

We draw lines in the air
And call them
Seconds, minutes, hours, days
And then we weave among them
Duties, dates,
Engagements, destinations,
Time frames, waits.
Held firmly in our schedules,
We swing serene above
All questions of the meaning of the universe,
Of why we are alive
And where is love.

8/15/88

Hunted

Thy footfall
Startles silences alive.
Shadowed,
They wait along the edge of life.
Thy passing presence
Springs them down the path
Racing and doubling
To escape the fate
Of coming face to face
With Love at last.

8/29/78

Prodigal

Come to myself, I trudge down distant roads.
Tired of the husks of life, I hurry home.
Knowing the cross awaits, I still must come,
Prepared to be a servant, not a son.

Your longing love outreaches me, outruns
My tardy progress borne on dragging feet.
Blessed, kissed, forgiven, lifted to my place,
I find the dreaded welcome sudden sweet.

Is this your punishment for sin, dear Lord?
The father's kiss? The ring? The robe? The calf?
Heart-heavy, I had feared repentance, Lord.
I came to cry, and now you tell me, "Laugh!"

8/18/78

A Timeless Marvel

You mean that I have always had forever?
I didn't need to scrabble, pinch and cheat,
To hoard the pennies of my days and never
Know that I held an endless balance sheet?

Looking for apples in my pleachéd garden,
Hearing time's winged chariot hurrying near,
I could not stop to pray or ask for pardon
Or help the fallen by the roadside here.

So, I come empty-handed, empty-hearted,
Without a wedding garment for your feast.
I had no time to change or get a present
Without a past or future or the least
Assurance that there would be world and time
Enough to finish even one small rhyme!

9/16/78

Repentance

My sin, however great,
Still cannot be
Greater than God's forgiveness.
There will,
I think there almost must be,
Pain—
The pain of knowing
How I've wounded Love.
And there must be
A turning back to Him.
Facing what I have done,
What I've become,
And seeing as He sees.

But, oh, then comes
The sinking to my knees
In joy and praise
That Love can love me still,
Can love and always has,
And always will.

8/24/92

Adamant

You are my rock.
I cling to the flinty face of your love,
Afraid, as always, of truth,
Unable, as usual, to believe
That tenderness can be stern.
I long for the softness of sand,
The treacherous self-indulgence
That washes beneath my discipline.
I hate and I need your hardness.
Help me to learn to love
The steady patience of stone,
The firmness, the reliability.

7/26/79

Mercy

I suppose I had to learn
I couldn't count
On them or me or anyone
To meet my deepest need
Before I would begin
To turn to Him.
But, when I came,
Reluctant,
Fighting the nature of reality,
Inclined to say,
"Don't think I'll kneel to You
Just because You are God,"
He overlooked my pride
And took me in
So that the long, slow healing
Could begin.

11/12/89

Rescued

Shepherd, my Shepherd,
Far have I strayed,
Lost to Your love for me,
Hurt and betrayed—
And yet Your love comes seeking.

Shepherd, my Shepherd,
I've been alone,
Bruising myself
On the shale and stone—
And still Your love comes seeking.

Shepherd, my Shepherd,
I've torn my fleece,
Caught in life's brambles,
Lost to Your peace—
And now Your love comes finding.

Shepherd, my Shepherd,
I'm in Your arms,
Safe from myself
And from evil's alarms—
And with Your love comes healing.

5/4/82

Comforter

Lord, do you wake at night
And hear your children crying?
And do you comfort them,
Warm-bosomed, mothering?

Do You hold them tenderly
Within the warmth of Your love
And soothe their fears and their sighing,
Until they relax in Your arms
And forget to weep
And sleep?

11/15/87

All There Is

I take the little scraps
Life offers me,
Embroider them
And sometimes add crochet
Where the edge is a little bit worn.

You look at my display
And sniff and look away
And say with scorn,
"Pathetic, isn't it!
If I couldn't do better than that,
I wouldn't bother to try."

But for some of us,
There is no alternative.
We have to take
What little we have
And try—
Or else we die.

3/16/88

Making Amends

What do You do
With the broken pieces, Lord?
The coat with crooked seams,
The pot that cracked,
The bankrupt business,
And the broken heart?
Is there for You
A point of no return
Or are these somewhere
Set apart, recycled
And redeemed?
Somehow, I dream
Of offering to You, Lord,
All that is smudged, spilled,
Blasted and blasphemed,
That by Your perfectness
They, too, may be restored.

10/3/80

Fish Wife

Can you use a fish wife, Lord?
My face, seamed with the sun,
My feet, splayed,
And my arms like shrunken rope?
My voice is harsh, Lord,
My speech is sharper than salt.
I smell of bilge water and brine.

Peace, woman!
Have you forgotten how it began,
How, long ago, I made friends
With a fisherman?

10/13/78

Appeal

Hey, Mister Jesus,
Hey, Mister Jesus,
Hey, Mister Jesus,
It's me!

Let's play together,
Let's stay together.
When we're together,
I'm free.

I know I'm sassy,
Street-wise and brassy,
Much too smart-assy
To be

Part of the church crowd,
Knees bent and heads bowed,
Everything done
Properly.

But, oh, Mr. Jesus,
Sweet Mr. Jesus,
Please save a minute
For me!

4/12/79

Anonymous

You were not a fat man, Lord,
Not rich, not powerful,
Did not grow old.
You had no sons,
No office in the town,
No honorary lectureship,
No cap and gown.
You were, of course,
The Word made flesh,
A humbling so immense
We could not see
Your kingliness
Without the world's regalia
Of power and pretense.

2/23/81

Establishment

They never just plain tell you
When you don't fit in.
Glances are sometimes exchanged
After something you've said.
Nothing overt, of course,
They're much too well bred.

They simply wait for you
To see your face
In the mirror of their manners
And their taste.
The process of revealing you to you
Proceeds apart from charity or haste.

You may find that you decide
To take your leave
A little earlier than you'd intended.
Somehow you feel reluctant to perceive
How mercilessly you have been befriended.

"Oh, must you go so soon?
Getting to know you
Really has been splendid."

3/27/80

Lawyer

The one was like a sparrow,
Hungry, brazen,
Hopping around the witnesses
And pecking them,
Snatching at pieces of the facts,
Crumbs that had somehow
Lost their truth,
Cocky and preening
As he tried to score.

The other, leonine,
A man of the establishment,
Not quite as deft
As might have been expected,
But able still
To put a sparrow in his place—
Outside the club.

After the trial,
The sparrow huddles small
Against a wall.
It would be cold again
Out on the pavement.

11/7/89

Person in Her Own Right

She had intended to have lived a life
Marked by small moments of success—
Her casseroles sought out at pot-luck suppers,
Hers, the best bread and the most towering cake,
Her kitchen floor, the cleanest
And her choice of drapes, so suitable.
She had expected friends
Who cherished both her kindness
And her wit,
Who sought her out for comfort and advice.
It would have been so nice
To have had friends . . .

And not this empty loneliness,
This corrugating grief.
Couldn't they understand
How desperately
She'd needed relief?

2/13/89 (*A reflection after hearing a monologue
by the alcoholic wife of an English vicar.*)

Busybody

As brisk and busy as a clock,
She drilled the marching minutes
Of her life.
Right march for housework;
Left for gardening.

So, forward through her days,
She stepped
Until her life wound down
And all her soldiers mutinied
And ran out of the hourglass.

Bereft of time,
She had to face eternity
Alone
With no troops left.

12/11/78

Isolated

It's lonely on a pedestal.
I know you wish me well
But being bronzed and set apart
Can be a kind of hell.

Perhaps it's easier for you
To think of me as carved in stone,
Noble and lofty and above
The need for human love.

But, if you really love me, dear,
Try to remember, I am here
In flesh as human and as tender
As yours—and not in statued splendor.

2/10/80

Friend in Need

You always seem to love the lumpy ones,
The people whose clothes don't fit quite right,
Who limp or mumble or squint . . .
The people who live in anonymous houses
On dingy streets,
Whose lives, however desperate and quiet,
Do not provoke them into riot.
They just keep taking the bus to work
And coming back home to eat
And to wish someone would phone.
Dear Lord, who fed the hungry,
Bless those who are alone.

2/11/80

Suicide

Oh, Em, how could you, dear?
Hiding from us
Who called ourselves your friends,
You grieved alone
Till loneliness destroyed you
And drove you to the horror of your end.

Where are you now?
The loveliness God made you
Should be a part
Of Heaven's high holy plan.
He calls you still.
Return to Him, dear wanderer!
The heart of God
Is not like that of man.

8/19/78

Deserted

The house of my heart is silent.
The rooms are shuttered and still.
The feelings you roused lie folded
Beside the window sill.

I shall return tomorrow,
Or after a decade or two,
To tidy up the sorrow
You left when you were through.

Now only ghosts of sunlight
Creep through the cracks and stand
Empty of motes and emotions
Where you once laid your hand.

3/29/79

Grief

Why did you die in autumn,
The first frost
Covering you
And covering my heart?
I need your warmth, my love!
The trees drop sadness.
I am a barren branch
Against a bitter sky.
Why did you die?

10/8/78

Farm Dog

The chain saw bites through the skin and flesh of the log.
The sawdust spills bright on the fallen snow,
Bright as the blood of the farmer's favorite dog
When she came staggering back from the road below.

She was already dying there at the door,
Still wagging her tail, still trusting his love to save her.
He had not known what kind of a morning chore
Awaited him. Still, he gave her
All of the love he could, called the vet,
Carried her out to the truck.

They sutured the gaping wound, but her heart gave out.
And now he is out in the woods in his old green coat
Tackling the logs for relief,
Sawing and sawing and sawing away at his grief.

11/21/78

Sharing

Meeting you on the stair
And telling you
The news we'd just received,
I saw your face break up
And crumble into tears.
Curious how I had not touched
My own grief yet,
Holding it far away from me,
Not giving it a place
Within my mind and heart
Until I shared the hurt with you
And saw your face.

8/14/90

Absence

It is the silence in the night
That breaks the heart—
The stillness
Where there should be breath,
Recalling emptiness and death.
One dreams of closely folded warmth
And wakes
To silence
And the loneliness it makes.

2/23/80

Grieving

I keep having to speak
Over this lump in my throat
And see through
This curtain of tears
And reach around and across
This mountain of pain
If I'm going to get in touch
With anyone again.

6/27/89

Waking Alone

It seems so strange
(Especially when I awake
From a late nap)
To find that you are gone.
It was not you who died
But Jack, our friend.
You still belong
Here, in the midst of life,
Here where I need you so.
The dusk falls
On a November afternoon
And I forgot to wake
To see you go—
Come quickly, love!
Come soon!
Do not be slow!

11/25/96

November

Goosefeather sky!
Feel the winter coming.
Goosefeather sky!
All the leaves fall down.

The snows of winter
Are whirring, humming;
They will cover the earth
With gray goose down.

Goosefeather sky!
All the grasses quiver,
The earth grows barren
And sere and brown.

Goosefeather sky!
How the branches shiver!
The birds have gone.
All the leaves fall down.

10/30/82

Epitaph

I hope it will be said
When I am dead,
"She wrote good poems
And she made good bread."

But let it not be said
Till I am dead.
To say it now
Would surely turn my head.

1/23/78